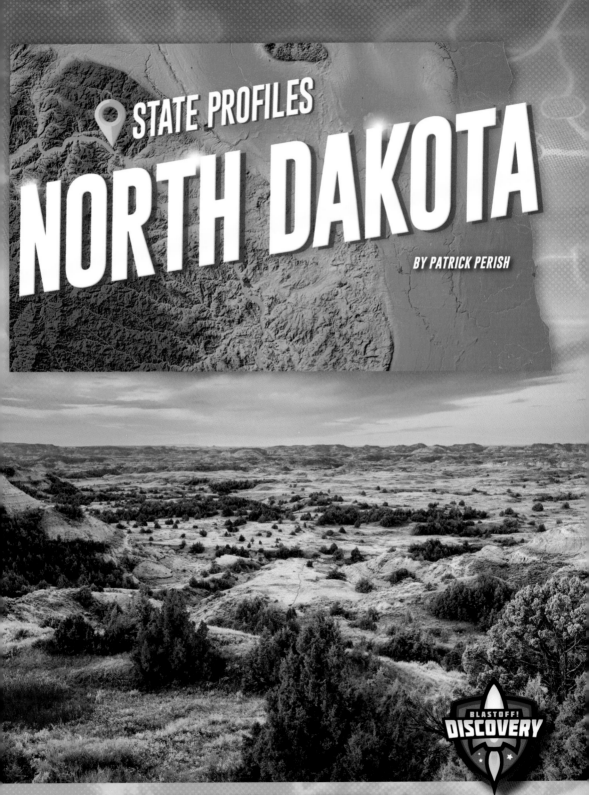

STATE PROFILES

NORTH DAKOTA

BY PATRICK PERISH

BELLWETHER MEDIA • MINNEAPOLIS, MN

Blastoff! Discovery launches a new mission: reading to learn. Filled with facts and features, each book offers you an exciting new world to explore!

BLASTOFF! UNIVERSE

BLASTOFF! Beginners — GRADE K

BLASTOFF! READERS — GRADES 1-3

BLASTOFF! DISCOVERY — GRADE 4

This edition first published in 2022 by Bellwether Media, Inc.

No part of this publication may be reproduced in whole or in part without written permission of the publisher.
For information regarding permission, write to Bellwether Media, Inc., Attention: Permissions Department,
6012 Blue Circle Drive, Minnetonka, MN 55343.

Library of Congress Cataloging-in-Publication Data

Names: Perish, Patrick, author.
Title: North Dakota / by Patrick Perish.
Description: Minneapolis, MN : Bellwether Media, Inc., 2022. | Series: Blastoff! Discovery: State profiles | Includes bibliographical references and index. | Audience: Ages 7-13 | Audience: Grades 4-6 | Summary: "Engaging images accompany information about North Dakota. The combination of high-interest subject matter and narrative text is intended for students in grades 3 through 8"– Provided by publisher.
Identifiers: LCCN 2021019667 (print) | LCCN 2021019668 (ebook) | ISBN 9781644873397 (library binding) | ISBN 9781648341823 (ebook)
Subjects: LCSH: North Dakota–Juvenile literature.
Classification: LCC F636.3 .P47 2022 (print) | LCC F636.3 (ebook) | DDC 978.4–dc23
LC record available at https://lccn.loc.gov/2021019667
LC ebook record available at https://lccn.loc.gov/2021019668

Editor: Colleen Sexton   Designer: Andrea Schneider

Printed in the United States of America, North Mankato, MN.

TABLE OF CONTENTS

THEODORE ROOSEVELT NATIONAL PARK

WHAT'S IN A NAME?

North Dakota is named for the Dakota people. The word *Dakota* means "friend."

The morning after a big rain, a park ranger drives out to check trail conditions in Theodore Roosevelt National Park. Her truck winds up the road. She passes quiet prairie dog towns and cottonwood trees growing in the lowlands. No one stirs in the campground.

INTERNATIONAL PEACE GARDEN

SALEM SUE

SHEYENNE NATIONAL GRASSLAND

TURTLE MOUNTAINS

LITTLE MISSOURI RIVER
THEODORE ROOSEVELT NATIONAL PARK

The ranger drives by steep slopes streaked with orange and red. She parks and hikes up a ridge. An old bison grazing at the top pays no attention to her. Wet **prairie** grasses glitter in the morning sun. Down below, swollen creeks rush to join the Little Missouri River. Welcome to North Dakota!

North Dakota is in the north-central United States. It is part of the **Midwest**. Montana lies to the west. South Dakota sits to the south. The Red River of the North forms the eastern border with Minnesota. North Dakota meets Canada to the north. The International Peace Garden is located on this border. It honors the friendship between Canada and the United States.

North Dakota covers 70,698 square miles (183,107 square kilometers). The Missouri River curves through western North Dakota. The capital, Bismarck, is in the south-central part of the state. Major cities Fargo and Grand Forks sit on the eastern border.

N
W + E
S

— MONTANA

IN THE MIDDLE

Rugby, North Dakota, has long been accepted as the geographic center of North America. However, recent research suggests it is farther south, in Center, North Dakota.

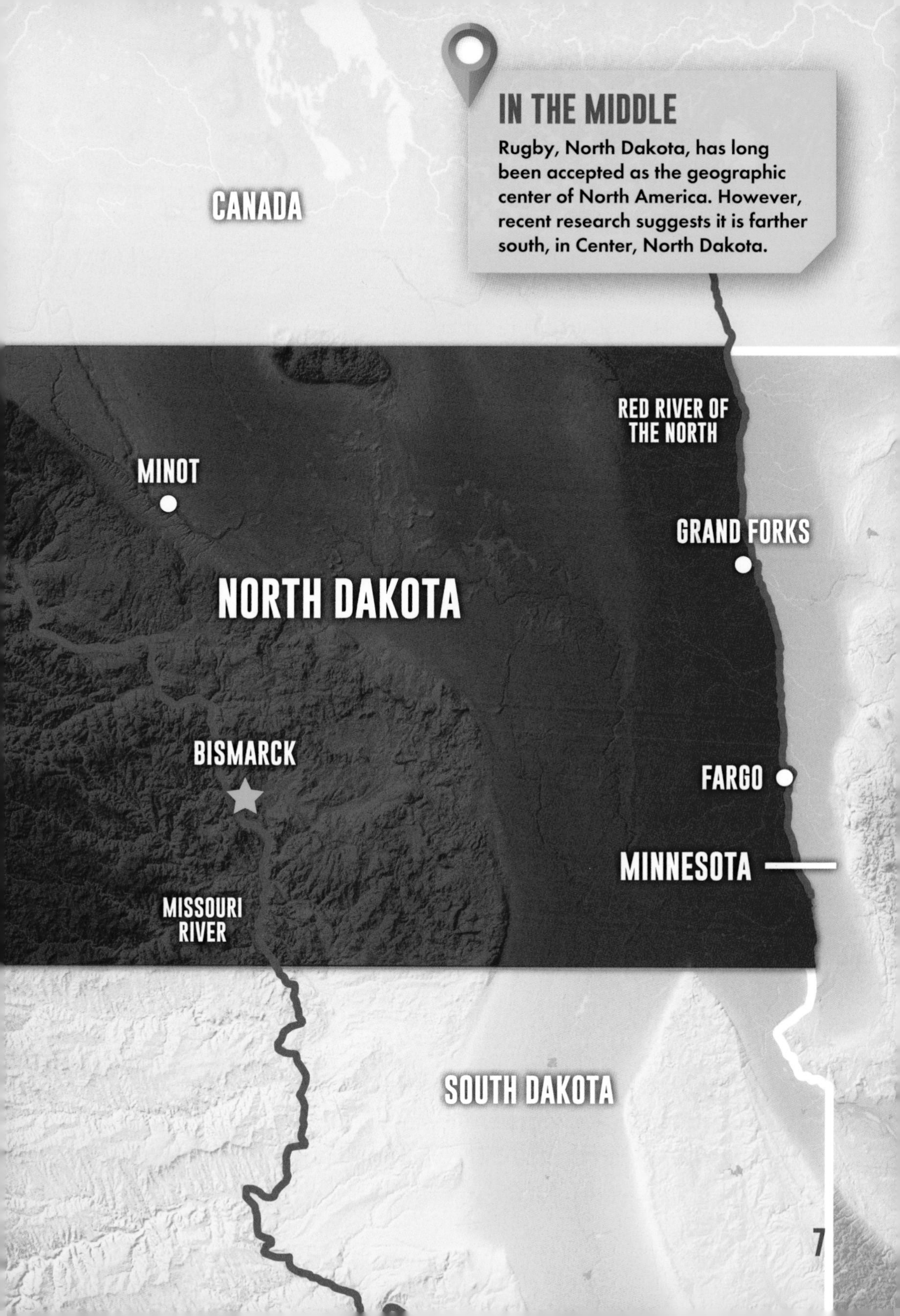

CANADA

RED RIVER OF
THE NORTH

MINOT

GRAND FORKS

NORTH DAKOTA

BISMARCK

FARGO

MINNESOTA

MISSOURI
RIVER

SOUTH DAKOTA

MANDAN CHIEF
LEADING EXPLORER

Humans entered North Dakota about 12,000 years ago. Over time, Native American groups formed. The Mandan, Hidatsa, and Arikara were farmers. The Chippewa fished, and the Lakota hunted bison. Europeans arrived in the 1700s. At different times, Spain and France claimed North Dakota.

The United States gained control of the land with the **Louisiana Purchase** in 1803. The government sent Meriwether Lewis and William Clark to explore the land. They followed the Missouri River into North Dakota in 1804. Thousands of **settlers** arrived during the 1870s seeking good farmland. They came from Norway, Germany, and eastern American states. North Dakota became the 39th state on November 2, 1889.

NATIVE PEOPLES OF NORTH DAKOTA

THE MANDAN, HIDATSA, AND ARIKARA TRIBES

- Original lands along the Missouri River in western North Dakota
- About 12,000 members enrolled
- Formed the Three Affiliated Tribes in 1862
- Arikara also called Sahnish

CHIPPEWA

- Original lands ranged from the Great Lakes to the Great Plains
- More than 30,000 members enrolled
- Also called Ojibwe and Anishinaabe

THE DAKOTA, LAKOTA, AND NAKOTA

- Original lands stretched from Minnesota to the Rocky Mountains
- More than 36,000 members enrolled
- Also called Sioux

LANDSCAPE AND CLIMATE

North Dakota is a state of wide-open spaces. The Red River Valley lies along the state's eastern edge. This low, flat land has rich soil. The **Great Plains** spread across most of North Dakota. Prairie grasses and farms cover flat stretches of land and gentle hills. Badlands rise in the southwest. Water and wind carved this colorful, rocky landscape.

MISSOURI RIVER

RED RIVER OF THE NORTH —

N W E S

RED RIVER VALLEY BADLANDS

GREAT PLAINS

A REAL HIGH POINT

North Dakota is not entirely flat. White Butte, the highest point, is 3,506 feet (1,069 meters) above sea level.

BADLANDS

SPRING
HIGH: 54°F (12°C)
LOW: 31°F (-1°C)

SUMMER
HIGH: 81°F (27°C)
LOW: 55°F (13°C)

FALL
HIGH: 55°F (13°C)
LOW: 31°F (-1°C)

WINTER
HIGH: 23°F (-5°C)
LOW: 3°F (-16°C)

°F = degrees Fahrenheit
°C = degrees Celsius

North Dakota's short summers are warm. Long hours of daylight make for good growing conditions. Strong winds blow thunderstorms across the prairie. Tornadoes sometimes touch down. Winters can be severely cold with fierce blizzards. Spring flooding is common in the river valleys.

A dazzling mix of plants and animals call North Dakota home. Pronghorn race across North Dakota's grasslands while greater prairie-chickens dance in the sea of golden grasses. Butterflies visit prairie roses, and bees buzz in the chokecherries. Meadowlarks hop along the ground looking for seeds. Bobcats hunt rabbits in the evenings.

Bighorn sheep and elk cross North Dakota's Badlands, and golden eagles soar overhead. Millions of **migrating** snow geese gather in wetlands. In the state's waters, northern pike dart after small fish and leeches.

PRONGHORN

BOBCAT

PRAIRIE DOGS

GOLDEN EAGLE

PRAIRIE DOG TOWNS

The underground tunnels of prairie dog towns crisscross the prairie. They connect areas for pups, places to sleep, and even bathrooms. Hundreds of prairie dogs may live in a single town!

Many of North Dakota's animals are losing their habitats as prairies are turned into farmland. Groups are working to preserve these homes to keep wildlife populations up.

GREATER PRAIRIE-CHICKEN

Life Span: up to 5 years
Status: vulnerable

greater prairie-chicken range = ■

LEAST CONCERN	NEAR THREATENED	VULNERABLE	ENDANGERED	CRITICALLY ENDANGERED	EXTINCT IN THE WILD	EXTINCT

With about 780,000 residents, North Dakota is one of the least populated states. It is also one of the most **rural** states. About two of every five North Dakotans live on farms and in small towns. The Red River Valley is the most populated part of the state.

NORTH DAKOTA'S FUTURE: AN AGING POPULATION

North Dakota's population is growing older. More than one of every four residents are age 55 or older. Providing care for the elderly will be a future challenge for the state.

FARGO

FAMOUS NORTH DAKOTAN

Name: Josh Duhamel

Born: November 14, 1972

Hometown: Minot, North Dakota

Famous For: Actor who has starred in many movies, including the *Transformers* movie series

Most North Dakotans have **ancestors** from Norway, Germany, and other European countries. Many Native Americans from the Chippewa, Dakota, and Three Affiliated Tribes live on **reservations**. Small numbers of Asian Americans, Black or African Americans, and Hispanic Americans call North Dakota home. Newcomers have arrived from the Philippines, Bhutan, Nepal, and Canada.

Bismarck was founded in 1872 as an army post on the Missouri River. The city grew into an early railroad **hub**. Today, it is a center for trade, transportation, and health care. It is also home to three colleges.

STANDING TALL

The 19-story capitol in Bismarck is the tallest building in the state.

Residents enjoy Bismarck's quiet parks and many bike trails. Its Dakota Zoo features tigers and colorful birds. Bismarck is in an area that is rich with history. The **Heritage** Center's exhibits cover **prehistoric** to **pioneer** times. In Fort Abraham Lincoln State Park just outside the city, Mandan earth lodges and a reconstructed fort are important educational sites.

HERITAGE CENTER

Farming was the first major industry in North Dakota. Today, most of its land is still used for farming. Top products include wheat, soybeans, sugar beets, and honey. Many farms raise beef cattle and bison. The state is also a leading producer of sunflowers.

MOOVE OVER HUMANS!

More than 1.8 million cattle live in North Dakota. That is more than double the number of people!

Oil was discovered in North Dakota in 1951. It is the state's leading mined product. Other major **natural resources** include soil, coal, clay, sand, and gravel. Most North Dakotans have **service jobs**. They work in health care, banking, education, and **tourism**. Factory workers make farm machinery, transportation equipment, and food products.

INVENTED IN NORTH DAKOTA

ROLL FILM
Date Invented: 1886
Inventor: David Houston

MR. BUBBLE BUBBLE BATH
Date Invented: 1961
Inventor: Harold Schafer

LICENSE PLATE TAGS
Date Invented: 20th century
Inventor: Lenard Milo Mennes

CREAM OF WHEAT CEREAL
Date Invented: 1893
Inventor: Tom Amidon

JELL-O SALAD

North Dakotans share many favorite dishes. Hot dish comes together in one pan. It features canned soup, meat, and vegetables. Taco-in-a-bag is made by opening a bag of chips and adding spicy taco meat. Cooks grill up bison burgers and sweet corn. Gravy poured over a hot beef sandwich is common on restaurant menus. Special occasions often include Jell-O salad with chunks of fruit and whipped cream.

Immigrants brought **traditional** foods that are still popular today. German-Russians introduced *knoephla*. This soup features dumplings, potatoes, and chicken. Icelandic *skyr* is a yogurt served with blueberries. Norwegians introduced a potato flatbread called *lefse*.

SKYR

SCANDINAVIAN LEFSE

4 SERVINGS

Have an adult help you make this traditional recipe!

INGREDIENTS

3 cups cooled mashed potatoes (instant are fine)

3 cups sifted flour

1 teaspoon salt

1 tablespoon sugar

2 tablespoons melted butter

2 tablespoons cream or half-and-half

DIRECTIONS

1. Mix all the ingredients in a large bowl.

2. Drop 1 tablespoon of dough at a time onto a floured surface. Roll out each ball into a thin circle.

3. On a preheated griddle, cook the lefse until a few light brown spots appear, and then flip.

4. Cool on dish towels.

5. To serve, spread with butter, sprinkle with sugar and cinnamon, and roll up.

CANYON OVERLOOK
THEODORE ROOSEVELT
NATIONAL PARK

Warm weather draws North Dakota's hikers and bikers to the state's many trails. Fishers reel in northern pike and walleyes. In the fall, hunters track deer, pheasants, and waterfowl. North Dakotans stay active in winter, too. Snowmobiling, snowboarding, and ice fishing are popular activities. College and high school sports bring out fans. Communities cheer on their football, basketball, volleyball, and hockey teams.

North Dakotans also enjoy the arts. Regional theaters put on lively plays and musicals. Local musicians perform across the state. Crafters show off their pottery, quilts, and other works at community festivals. Galleries feature artwork inspired by North Dakota's beautiful landscapes.

THE ENCHANTED HIGHWAY

Huge sculptures of people and animals tower over a highway in western North Dakota. These scrap metal statues make a quiet rural area feel magical.

NOTABLE SPORTS TEAM

University of North Dakota Fighting Hawks

Sport: National Collegiate Athletic Association hockey

Started: 1946

Place of Play: Ralph Engelstad Arena

North Dakotans are a tight-knit community. Their traditions and festivals bring them together. The Red River Valley Fair takes place in West Fargo. This six-day summer festival features farm exhibits, rides, music, and food. **Powwows** celebrate Native American **cultures** through traditional songs and dances. The United Tribes Powwow draws crowds to Bismarck every September.

UNITED TRIBES
POWWOW

A WILD WEST CELEBRATION

Performers at the Medora Musical bring the Old West to life! This show celebrates 26th president Theodore Roosevelt who spent time hunting and ranching in North Dakota in the 1880s.

MEDORA MUSICAL

Rodeos fill arenas throughout the state. Riders compete in horse jumping, roping, and bull riding. In fall, Minot holds Norsk Høstfest. It is the largest Scandinavian festival in the country. It features a Viking village and a lefse-making contest. There is plenty to celebrate in the great state of North Dakota!

NORSK HØSTFEST

25

1738

European fur traders begin exploring North Dakota and meet Native Americans

1878

New railroads and available land begin a wave of settlers called the Great Dakota Boom

1804

Sacagawea joins the Lewis and Clark expedition in North Dakota

1803

The Louisiana Purchase adds what is now North Dakota to the United States

1812

The first permanent European settlement in the area is established at Pembina

1947
Theodore Roosevelt
National Park is established

2000s
An oil-mining boom begins
in western North Dakota

1997
Historic floods occur in
the Red River Valley,
and much of Grand
Forks is damaged

2016
Protesters oppose
construction of an oil pipeline
under the Missouri River
near Standing Rock Indian
Reservation, but the pipeline
is completed in 2017

1889
North Dakota becomes
the 39th state

Nicknames: The Peace Garden State, The Sioux State, The Roughrider State, The Flickertail State

Motto: Liberty and Union Now and Forever, One and Inseparable

Date of Statehood: November 2, 1889 (the 39th state)

Capital City: Bismarck ★

Other Major Cities: Fargo, Grand Forks, Minot

Area: 70,698 square miles (183,107 square kilometers); North Dakota is the 19th largest state.

Population
779,094
(2020)

STATE FLAG

North Dakota adopted its flag in 1911. On a blue background, an eagle holds an olive branch and arrows in its claws. It clutches a banner in its mouth that displays the motto of the United States, *E Pluribus Unum*, meaning "Out of many, one." A rising sun and 13 stars are arranged above the eagle. Under the eagle is a banner that reads *North Dakota*.

INDUSTRY

Main Exports

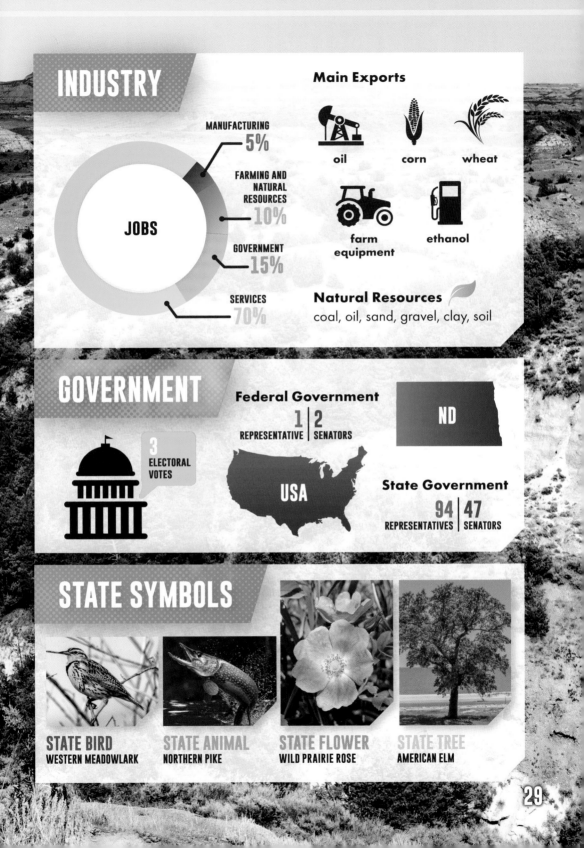

JOBS

MANUFACTURING
5%

FARMING AND NATURAL RESOURCES
10%

GOVERNMENT
15%

SERVICES
70%

oil

corn

wheat

farm equipment

ethanol

Natural Resources
coal, oil, sand, gravel, clay, soil

GOVERNMENT

Federal Government

1 REPRESENTATIVE | **2** SENATORS

3 ELECTORAL VOTES

USA

ND

State Government

94 REPRESENTATIVES | **47** SENATORS

STATE SYMBOLS

STATE BIRD
WESTERN MEADOWLARK

STATE ANIMAL
NORTHERN PIKE

STATE FLOWER
WILD PRAIRIE ROSE

STATE TREE
AMERICAN ELM

GLOSSARY

ancestors—relatives who lived long ago

cultures—beliefs, arts, and ways of life in places or societies

Great Plains—a region of flat or gently rolling land in the central United States

heritage—the traditions, achievements, and beliefs that are part of the history of a group of people

hub—a center of activity

immigrants—people who move to a new country

Louisiana Purchase—a deal made between France and the United States; it gave the United States 828,000 square miles (2,144,510 square kilometers) of land west of the Mississippi River.

Midwest—a region of 12 states in the north-central United States

migrating—traveling from one place to another, often with the seasons

natural resources—materials in the earth that are taken out and used to make products or fuel

pioneer—related to people who are among the first to explore or settle in an area

powwows—Native American gatherings that usually include dancing

prairie—related to a large, open area of grassland

prehistoric—the span of time before humans had writing systems

reservations—areas of land that are controlled by Native American tribes

rural—related to the countryside

service jobs—jobs that perform tasks for people or businesses

settlers—people who move to live in a new, undeveloped region

tourism—the business of people traveling to visit other places

traditional—related to customs, ideas, or beliefs handed down from one generation to the next

AT THE LIBRARY

Cooke, Tim. *Sacagawea*. New York, N.Y.: Gareth Stevens, 2017.

Maine, Tyler. *North Dakota*. North Mankato, Minn.: Capstone Press, 2017.

Squire, Ann O. *North Dakota*. New York, N.Y.: Children's Press, 2019.

ON THE WEB

FACTSURFER

Factsurfer.com gives you a safe, fun way to find more information.

1. Go to www.factsurfer.com.

2. Enter "North Dakota" into the search box and click Q.

3. Select your book cover to see a list of related content.

INDEX